AF211745

LOU IRVIN

SNAPCHAT

**The Ultimate Guide to SnapChat Marketing,
Discover How to Use SnapChat for Marketing
and Earn Profits**

Descrierea CIP a Bibliotecii Naționale a României
LOU IRVIN
   SNAPCHAT. The Ultimate Guide to SnapChat Marketing,
Discover How to Use SnapChat for Marketing and Earn Profits /
Lou Irvin – Bucharest: Editura My Ebook, 2021
   ISBN

LOU IRVIN

SNAPCHAT

The Ultimate Guide to SnapChat Marketing, Discover How to Use SnapChat for Marketing and Earn Profits

My Ebook Publishing House
Bucharest, 2021

CONTENTS

Contents

SnapChat As a Marketing Tool

The growing use of the internet has prompted a shift in the nature in which businesses seek to promote their products and services. The use of social media has also gone a long way in increasing internet participation amongst people across all divides. One of the many social mediaplatforms called Snapchat is a multimedia mobile application focused on image messaging.

Internet users, especially social media users, have devised ingenious ways of drawing traffic to respected sites for a number of reasons. Today, social media is a vital tool for internet marketing. Businesses, both small and big, have switched to internet as their primary platform for marketingtheir goods and services. This report therefore provides an in-depth analysis of Snapchat as one of the many social media platforms and illuminates how this platform is currently used by internet marketers for the purpose of brand awareness.

SnapChat As a Social Media Platform

One ought to note that Snapchat is principally used to create multimedia messages that are commonly referred to as snaps. On most occasions, snaps are images that can be manipulated to amalgamate various effects as preferred by the user. Nonetheless, snaps can also consist of short videos and drawings that are also editable to contain captions, effects and filters. Over the years, Snapchat has evolved significantly to include new and interesting features that add to user experience. Today, this mobile application is not only used for socialization but also as a marketing tool for most businesses that seek to attain online awareness amongst its potential and existing customers.

There are a number of feature incorporated in Snapchat that makes it ideal for use as not only a social media platform but also a marketing tools for businesses that seek awareness online. For example, one of Snapchat's features called the

8

Geofilter was incorporated in the application in 2014. This feature is important for availing certain special graphic overlays when the user of theapplication is in a certain geographical place like a city or event. As such, users are able to identify with their locations when they take snaps of images of videos of their surroundings.

Another significant feature of Snapchat is the 'Lens' feature that was first introduced in 2015. This is a special feature that provides users with the opportunity of adding real time effects in thesnaps of images or videos that they take. One ought to note that this feature makes use of face detection technology that also forms a vital part of the Snapchat application. When using the lensfeature, Snapchat users activate the face detection technology by a long-press on a face that appears within the view-finer window or screen. These are just some of the features that together bring up the much needed user experience and satisfaction.

Unlike many social media platforms and application, Snapchat is user-friendly and offers real time guidance to users during use. When it comes to synchronizing contacts, Snapchat offers oneof the best and easy-to-use guides. Snapchat users are able to synchronize their contacts from other social media platforms that they already have. Additionally, Snapchat also suggests contacts to its users. As such, Snapchat users are able to link up with contacts that they might know or be interested in. in addition to the provisions of contacts, one ought to note that Snapchat also features notifications of snaps that can be customized according to user preferences. One is able to customize his or her image or short video in a way that it can be viewed for a specified period before it becomes inaccessible to other users. On most occasions, a period between one and ten seconds is provided. Users are therefore able to make their snaps viewable to others for a specified time between one and ten seconds.

Initially, users were required to hold down the screen as a way of being able to view a snap in the form of a short video or image. However, this is no longer the case. This option was excluded from the Snapchat application in 2015. According to the brains behind Snapchat, the requirement to hold down the screen as an option that allows users to view snaps was aimed at frustrating the ability of users to take screenshots of images or short videos. It should be noted that Snapchat does not deter the taking of screenshots. However, it is able to notify the original sender of a snap that a screenshot of his or her snap has been saved. Alongside being able to customize the period that a snap can be made available, it is also important to note that one snap

10

can be replayed on a daily basis for free. Nonetheless, if users require more replays they have to purchase them with the help of micro-transactions that are provided in the user interface of Snapchat.

Just like any other social media platform, Snapchat has a provision of adding friends via phone contacts and usernames. This is called synchronization. The ability to add friends is made a lot easier through the 'Add Nearby' function or customizable snap-codes that allow users to link upwith their contacts that are available on other social media platforms that they might already have. Unlike numerous common social media platforms, the intention of Snapchat was to counteract the norm in which social media users were forced to deal with an idealized social media identity of themselves; which was described as having denied internet users the ability toenjoy their communications in social media.

Another interesting feature of Snapchat application is the 'Memories' feature that was introduced in July 2016. This feature was perhaps the one last component that was lacking in the application to make it absolutely perfect. Since the introduction of this feature, Snapchat users are now able to save story posts and snaps into private storage areas. As such, these images and short videos can be viewed remotely together with other snaps that are stored in the device. In addition to that, these snaps can be edited and most importantly published again in order to be redisplayed inSnapchat.

In addition to being able to save previous snaps using Snapchat, one is also able to search the saved content by their dates or with the help of an object recognition system. Those snaps that are made accessible through 'Memories' can also be locked and a 'My Eyes Only' area. One ought to note that this option is made available for users who seek to save snaps but also keep them out of reach of other people that might have access to their devices. When locked, these stored saps can only be accessed after keying in a PIN that is set by the original user of the application. According to the brains behind the Snapchat application stated that the idea of 'Memories' as a feature of Snapchat was inspired by the common practice of people having to physically scroll through their photos in their phones with a bid to show them to their friends.

SnapChat For Business

The core value of most businesses is to connect with their target audience for their goods and services in the most convenient way. Businesses make use of a number of marketing strategies in order to meet their target margins. Snapchat can now be considered as one of the platforms that internet marketers an businesses can use to take their marketing and businesses to the next level when it comes reaching their potential consumers. While the use of Snapchat for the purpose of marketing and connecting with consumers can feel overwhelming for internet marketers and businesses, one should note that it is always gainful to come up with an effective platform that offers opportunities of connecting with target audiences. It is only through this that marketers and businesses are able to keep their clients, acquire new clients and sell more.

According to the statistics of the volume of Snapchat users on a daily basis, it is beyond doubts that this application can be valuable when it comes to being used as a marketing tool for business. On most occasions, a marketing platform is identified by its ability to reach a wide base of people ad users. According to recent statistics, Snapchat is accessed by over forty one percent of all adults in the United States of America alone. These statistics alone should impress any marketer of business in this nation. Aside from that, one should note that Snapchat receives millions of new subscribers on a daily basis over the world half of whom are aged above twenty five years.

A platform like Snapchat that has more than half of its users aged above 25 years is a significant tool that can be used by internet marketers and businesses to further their agendas. There are a number of reasons for this. First of all, users above this age are considered as mature and able to understand the direction of their economies in terms of the goods and service that trend. This is an important aspect for marketers. Businesses and marketers target people that are able to understand the values of whatever goods and services on sale.

Secondly, people aged above 25 years form a greater percentage of consumers or rather buyers of goods and services marketed in the internet. It becomes therefore very imperative for internet marketers to direct their attention towards marketing platforms that has an audience aged above 25 years. These are

14

the actual buyers of such goods and services. The ability of Snapchat to attract an audience of this nature makes it and invaluable tool for internet marketers and businesses.

Facts and Figures For SnapChat Business

The biggest advantage that has come with cyber world is the ability to get exact figures of the number of internet users at a given time and the sites they visit. This therefore makes it easy for analysts to come up with the exact figures of internet users that visit given sites at given times. As such, the number of Snapchat users can readily be identified for the purpose of ascertaining whether it can be an invaluable tool for marketing. Aside from the statistics, there are also a number of advantages Snapchat has over other social media platforms that are also praised worldwide as good marketing platforms for businesses and internet marketers.

Snapchat's Statistics

There have always been contradictions of figures and statistics of active users on not only Snapchat but other social media platforms as well. However, estimated statistics indicate that Snapchat has over 200 million active users on a monthly basis. These active users have been found to send over 700 million snaps in the form of short videos and photos on a daily basis. These snaps receive over 500 million viewers on a daily basis. These statistics alone are enough to verify that any business or internet markets with the aim of obtaining audience for their products and services are able to meet this objective through engaging gin Snapchat.

It is estimated that over 100 million users are active on Snapchat daily from all over the world. Recent statistics have also indicated that Snapchat reaches close to 12 percent of the entire digital world of the United States of America. This percentage might not seem as much until one takes into consideration how much the actual population of the US amounts to. When this is looked into keenly, 11 or 12% is still a decent figure to work with.

Snapchat is a mobile application that is downloaded from plays stores of android and windows devices. This function is able to tell exactly how many Snapchat apps are downloaded.

According to statistics, Snapchat was amongst 13 most downloaded apps from windows and android devices all over the world in 2015. Besides that, Snapchat would most of the time appear in the top three amongst video and photo applications downloaded all over the world.

One of the major reasons that Snapchat would be considered as an invaluable internet marketing tools if the exponential growth it has exhibited in the few years it has been in operation. Recent researches have indicated that Snapchat grew as much in only a year as twitter did in over four years. As a matter of fact, Snapchat is considered as having more users as compared to twitter; one of the many social media platforms available. This qualifies Snapchat as a major player in cyber world an especially as far as internet marketing and social media are concerned.

It is also important to note that over 76% of social media users on Snapchat are online shoppers as well. Online shopper can best be described as internet users who make use of the internet as an avenue of finding goods and services that they can finally purchase and consume.

18

Furthermore, Snapchat users have been found to spend an average of half an hour per day in the application. This is an indication that all Snapchat users find enough time to go through the contents and information share on it by other users. The fact that Snapchat exhibits over 100 million active users on a daily basis and 76% of these users are online shoppers only leaves one wondering how big the audience for internet marketers and online-based businesses.

The Advantages of Limited Competition

It is important to note that every business that has ever existed and made good profits must have had social media presence at one point. This includes presence on Facebook, Instagram and twitter amongst many other social media platforms available. On most occasions, however, it isdifficult to stand out or connect with people on such platforms. This is especially because of the level of competition for businesses on social media. Every business wants to be felt son social media to an extent that it is very overwhelming for users. They are kept confused of which marketer or online-based business to give more attention.

Even though Snapchat is exhibiting enormous popularity amongst similar brands rapidly, one ought to note that there is still limited competition for businesses that seek online awareness through this platform. Unlike other social media platforms like twitter and Facebook that businesses and online marketers have flocked with the intention of gaining online existence, Snapchat is yet to be fully exploited fully as a marketing platform. Snapchat therefore become one of the few social media platforms that has a wide range of audience but only a limited number of businesses trying to exploit such audiences for business growth.

SnapChat is Comparatively Different

When confronted with the idea of social media, many immediately think of a site in which people connect with the purpose of communicating through written messages. However, Snapchat is totally different. Snapchat users share snaps in the form of short videos and images that are edited with numerous pictorial effects. As such, users meet new audiences in a completely new way with the help of completely new content. Just as it is the norm, internet users are always enthusiastic about new stuff and are more likely to engage in new and differentstuff as compared to ordinary things that they are used to on a daily basis.

The fact that Snapchat offers a completely different user experience as compared to other formsof social media platforms makes it stand out. This is a big advantage for entrepreneurs who seek online awareness and attention through this site. Though many might not immediately ascertain the level to which Snapchat can assist their internet marketing intentions and aspirations, it is worth noting that the exiting audience in Snapchat alone is enough to convince an internet marketer or an online-based business of gainful platform to market their goods and services.

Snapchat offers a feeling of authenticity

One ought to note that social media sited are generally great when it comes to rapport building. On most occasions, social media sites play an imperative role in making their users view online- based businesses from the exact perspectives they would like to be viewed from. Despite being considered as one of the many social media sites, Snapchat amplifies the idea of social media marketing.

Unlike many social media sites, Snapchat tends to promote what is happening now. The use of modified images and videos communicate current undertakings in a way that makes their viewers to instantly understand whatever is being communicated. The fact that Snapchat allows its users to edit photos with the help of filters with the aim of making them more appealing and interesting brings a completely different user experience as compared to the rest of social mediasites.

Snapchat is free

This might not be the single most important aspect of marketing through Snapchat but we certainly cannot go without acknowledging the fact that it is free. This is perhaps the only advantage for internet marketing sites that cuts across the board on equal dimensions for all the sites. Therefore, the fact that Snapchat is free to download does not make so much significance until topped up with other advantages that come with it including less competition and authenticity.

The demographics of Snapchat

There is nothing as important as the demographics of an online marketing platform for online- based businesses. It is only through the demographics that a business is able to ascertain whether the site selected for its marketing is viable for the kind of products and services it offers. It is therefore imperative to take into close consideration the demographics of any online marketing site as a way of aligning the interned goods and services to the right audience and most especially consumers. It is only this way that an effective marketing strategy can be developed and actualized.

According to recent statistics, over 60% of smart phone owners aged between 13 and 34 yearsold in the United States of America use Snapchat. This is an implication that more than half of smart phone owner in USA are active users of Snapchat. On most occasions, USA is used as a point of reference in order to estimate the percentage of users across the globe. Therefore, it is worth noting that half of smart phone owners cut across the world make use of Snapchat.

Out of the total number of Snapchat users, recent statistical analysis validated in 2015 indicate that 37% fall in the age bracket of 8-24 years. The statistics also show that 71% of Snapchat users are below 25 years. A close evaluation of these figures illuminates the kind of audience expected in the event that an online marketer or an online-based business takes up Snapchat as one of its fundamental marketing platforms. The statistics can readily tell the kind of audience expected and the nature of response anticipated when marketing commences on this platform. The population of Snapchat users comprises of 30% men and 70% women. This is an important revelation because it shows the gender distribution of Snapchat users. There are online-based businesses on internet marketers who majorly target ladies while other target men. It is thus important to know the gender distribution of a prospected marketing site before embarking on the actual marketing.

According to a recent study, Snapchat has a younger audience as compared to a number of similar social media sites. Despite being described as a younger audience, more than half of Snapchat's users are above the age of 25. People that fall within this age bracket form the biggestpercentage of consumers of any commodity or service across the globe. This is because this age bracket forms the largest population in the world when analyzed through a global census. In addition to that, the largest percentage of people with salaries, either from formal or informal employment, fall within this age bracket. This is an implication that the largest percentage of people with the financial capability of buying goods and services are aged above 25. Thus, the fact that more of Snapchat's users fall within this age bracket makes Snapchat an invaluable marketing tool for not only online marketers but also online-based businesses that seek to have online awareness.

How to Utilize SnapChat As a Marketing Tool

Snapchat is an invaluable tool that offers a myriad of marketing options that can be exploited in order to meet certain goals and objectives of a business. Businesses that seek online awareness through Snapchat have since devised ingenious ways of drawing attention to their posts or snaps. It turn, they have gained significantly especially because of the massive audience available at Snapchat. The very its step to create online awareness through Snapchat is definitely to install a Snapchat app in your device. This will thus enable the posting and subsequent viewing of snaps. Additionally, this also helps a lot in understanding the trends in Snapchat and the features that are more likely to woe viewers more.

Online-based businesses or internet marketers are able to come up with creative Snap Ads, build impressive Sponsored Geofilters or offer their customers a chance to interact effectively with Sponsored Lens. These are new terms for those that are not familiar with Snapchat. Nonetheless, they are some of the most effective strategies that online-based businesses are able to implementin a bid to promote their products and services to existing and potential customers. These strategies are discussed further below.

The use of Snap Ads as a strategy for building brand awareness

The use of Snap Ads is an effective way of catching the attention of prospected audience. A Snap Ad is merely a 10-second video always incorporated in stories and appears full screen. These short videos are meant to enhance user experience by giving them an opportunity to swipe up with the aim of viewing more detailed contents. Such content may include articles, mobile websites, long videos and even app install Ads. On most occasions, viewers of Snapchat stories find it interesting to view stories that are combined with short videos that enhance their experience. It is for this reason that Snapchat users, especially marketers, are advised to incorporate such ads in a bid to capture the attention of their viewers while attempting topromote an item or service through Snapchat.

Snap Ads are an effective means of making posts or snaps more lucrative on Snapchat because of the swipe-up speed. According to a recent discovery, the swipe-up rate for the Snap Ads was found to be five times higher as compared to the ordinary click-through rates on other social media platforms. This is a great advantage for Snapchat users because through this, they are able to go through more videos and other related content in a short period as compared to when they do the same on other social media sites. This is thus an invaluable means of attracting viewers to a given snap and subsequently promoting products and services to a larger audience.

A case study on the use of Snap Ads

One of the most popular music app known as the Spotify bought Snap Ads with the intention of promoting its annual 'Year in Music' campaign. This is a campaign in which Spotify users are able to view the total number and the genres of songs they have listened to on Spotify the entireyear. This strategy was a success as the Ads of Spotify popped up on the Discovery Channel of Snapchat during which it highlighted different music genres every day. As a result of this initiative, Spotify was able to earn twenty six million views. As if that is not enough, the music app also experienced a 30% increase on the number of subscribers. This was a significant increase. Since then, the mobile app has continued using Snap Ads and has, as a matter of fact, spiced up its marketing strategies on Snapchat using other means. If the use of Snap Ads was able to catapult Spotify to a different level as far as marketing of its product was concerned then it is almost definite that this strategy is valid for internet marketing.

Building impressive Sponsored Geofilters for promotion on Snapchat

Georfilter is one of Snapchat's features that were incorporated into the app in 2014. This feature is important for availing certain special graphic overlays when the user of the application is in a certain geographical place like a city or event. As such, users are able to identify with their locations when they take snaps of images of videos of their surroundings. There are two different types of Geofilters that can be utilized by businesses to take their marketing to the next level.

One of the Geofilters is known as the On-Demand Geofilter that can be bought from as little as $5. The other one is the Sponsored Geofilter that is much more expensive and would ordinarycost from hundreds to thousands of dollars.

It is noteworthy that Geofilters have recently proven to be invaluable when it comes to uplifting new online-base businesses. They are always seen as small art graphics that usually appear over a snap. When Snapchat users in a given location take and post snaps, they are able to select specific Geofilters and use them to communicate where they are and at what time. One ought to note that these Geofilters can also be used by Snapchat users to explain the reasons why they took the snaps and the geographical location in which the snaps were taken.

A good example of the use of Georfilters on Snapchat is when a taco truck has a Cinco de Mayo even somewhere, Snapchat users are able to take snaps as they eat tacos and include fun geofilters. These geofilters will in turn show their friends where they are taking the snaps from. Additionally, the geofilters are also able to tell whose tacos the Snapchat users are eating thereby helping in not only promoting the event but also the tacos being consumed at the event. In such ascenario, a less expensive On-Demand geofilter will be sufficient.

In the event that a campaign is less specific when it comes to location, say a nationwide campaign, Snapchat users in the entire nation are able to take snaps that show them appreciating the national event and subsequently add filters over it. It is during such scenarios that Sponsored

Geofilters are used. This strategy is highly effective because it has been noted that such a nationwide campaign is able to meet an estimated 40 to 60% of daily Snapchat users within a given country. This big percentage of audience reached is the reason why sponsored Geofilters can cost up to thousands of dollars.

A case study of the use of Sponsored Geofilters as a marketing strategy for businesses

During an event to commemorate Worlds AIDS day, RED (a non-profit organization) partnered with Snapchat to help spread the word about the event. The duo created two Geofilters that Snapchat users could use to exhibit their support for the event. Every time a Snapchat user sent any of the Geofilters, Bill and Melinda Gates Foundation donated a sum of $3 to the non-profit organization RED to assist in the fight against the deadly disease. Over $3 million was collected for the campaign.

It is worth noting that about 14 Snapchat users got involved in the campaign through Snapchat. Out of the total number of Snapchat users involved, 97% of them were aged between 13 and 34 years. In addition, more than two thirds of the total number of Snapchat users who involved themselves in the campaign remembered the campaign against AIDS. As if that was not enough, Snapchat users who saw the filters correctly were 90% likely to offer donations to RED to assist in their campaign. According to the statistics indicated in this case study one can comfortably deduce that the use of Sponsored Georfilters in Snapchat can go a long way in assisting internet marketers and online-based businesses to attain the much desired online awareness.

The use of Sponsored Lens as a strategy for building brand awareness

One ought to note that Sponsored Lenses provide Snapchat users with the opportunity of playing around with the Snaps they have created. Sponsored Lenses enhance user experience while using Snapchat and are activated by merely pressing and holding on the faces on their screens. They come with an array of lenses including raising eyebrows that eventually trigger animations. The lenses therefore give users the opportunity of customizing their snaps with the aim of meeting their own desires and satisfaction.

Once a Snapchat user had customized his or her snaps with the help of Sponsored Lenses, they are able to instantly send them to their friends or even post them to their stories. It has been noted that customized saps using Sponsored lenses are not difficult to create as was thought. On average, Snapchat users spend approximately 20 seconds to customize their snaps with the help of the Sponsored Lenses. This is quite doable and it is therefore advisable for Snapchat users to make use of it effectively in order to draw more attention and subsequently more traffic to their snaps.

The biggest advantage that has come with cyber world is the ability to get exact figures of the number of internet users at a given time and the sites they visit. This therefore makes it easy for analysts to come up with the exact figures of internet users that visit given sites at given times. As such, the number of Snapchat users can readily be identified for the purpose of ascertaining whether it can be an invaluable tool for marketing. Aside from the statistics, there are also a number of advantages Snapchat has over other social media platforms that are also praised worldwide as good marketing platforms for businesses and internet marketers.

According to the marketing strategies discussed above, one can immediately notice that all are chargeable. This is an im0lication that internet marketers and online-based businesses who seek to create brand awareness on Snapchat through these means will have to pay considerable amounts of cash in order to succeed. Nonetheless, it should be noted that not all such businesses or marketers are willing or able to make such payments as quoted. This is not a major challenge. There are other ways of creating brand awareness on Snapchat without spending evenmoney.

Non-paid strategies of creating brand awareness on Snapchat Provide incentives

The core value of most businesses is to connect with their target audience for their goods and services in the most convenient way. Businesses make use of a number of marketing strategies in order to meet their target margins. Snapchat can now be considered as one of the platforms that internet marketers an businesses can use to take their marketing and businesses to the next level when it comes reaching their potential consumers. While the use of Snapchat for the purpose of marketing and connecting with consumers can feel overwhelming for internet marketers and businesses, one should note that it is always gainful to come up with an effective platform that offers opportunities of connecting with target audiences. It is only through this that marketers and businesses are able to keep their clients, acquire new clients and sell more. An added advantage is always the use of incentives.

Incentives are an effective way of creating brad loyalty for any business without taking much consideration of the marketing platform used. This definitely works for Snapchat marketers as well. Offering incentives on Snapchat is quite a challenges and hence users must device critical measured of ensuring that their incentives work. This is because snaps not only disappear after they have been watched by a Snapchat user but are also available for only 24 hours. This is an implication that Snapchat must vigilantly follow snaps if they want a piece of the incentives thatare offered on this social media platform.

Case Study 1

During an incentive for food delivery service, Grubhub hosted a scavenger hunt that lasted a whole week. The hunt, dubbed SnapHunt, posted a new challenge every day for seven days. Those who successfully completed the challenges were given a free takeout worth $50.

According to the statistics collected after the hunt, more than thirty percent of Grubhub followers on Snapchat actively participated in the hunt. At the end of the week long campaign, the brand registered a 20% growth in the number of its followers on Snapchat. Therefore, one ought to be cognizant of the fact that the use of incentives as a marketing strategy on Snapchat is able to increase brand awareness and subsequently lead to significant increase in sales for any business. **Tell an impressive story on the snaps posted on Snapchat**

As it has been noted already, snaps are merely stories that are told in the form of images and short videos and last for only

24 hours. On ordinary occasions, social media users are attracted to impressive stories. As a matter of fact, users of social media only take time to react to posts or stories that appeal to them. It is from this perspective that online-based businesses and internet marketers should base their marketing tips. For a story to sell it must be great and appealing to its viewers of readers. It is therefore imperative for marketers who seek brand awareness on Snapchat to come up with impressive stories that can capture the attention of their follows. In the event that a business keep posting meaningless and flat stories, it is likely to be disregarded by its followers for having not taste when it comes to its postings.

Case Study 2

A candy company called the Sour Patch Kids had an intention of attracting more teenage consumers and resorted to sending cute characters 'Sweet' and 'Sour'. This was during a quest that was done in collaboration with an internet personality known as Logan Paul. The company came up with an impressive snap that narrated a story of Sweet and Sour embarrassing Logan. Atthe end of the narrative, one of them got lost in the city thereby showing an impressive suspense of teenagers.

At the end of the first story, the candy company managed to get 583k views. Surprisingly, the number of views shot to over 6.8 million at the end of the fifth story. This implied that Snapchatusers were continually interested in the stories narrated by the campaign. At the end of the campaign, Sur Patch Kids was able to register 120,000 new followers. This is thus a confirmation that telling a great story on snaps can further a business's marketing agenda to thenext level.

Hire the best talent

As a social media platform, Snapchat is an invaluable avenue to advertise vacancies in a company or business. In 2015, AOL had an intention of increasing the total number of Millennial women amongst its staff and opted to make use of Snapchat in this quest. In an attempt to meet this objective, the company ran two Snapchat videos that lasted ten seconds each. The first video was meant to promote BuiltbyGirls; a program that invested in startups that were led by women. The other one was a footage that showed employees of AOL at work. At the end of the week long campaign, 17 million views were generated. As a result, the number of expected applications rose by 18 percent.

Offer access to live events

It is worth noting that Snapchat is an effective platform for real-time marketing on social media. This is because it is capable of offering its audience the chance to access live events as they happen. Businesses can take advantage of this provision to take their promotion further in a bid to reach more people and subsequently register more sales for their products and services. It should be noted that promotion of live events on Snapchat can be used during product launches or even trade shows.

There is nothing as important in marketing as offering something new and unique to potential clients. People find it interesting to be involved in something new and unique. It is for this reasonthat businesses ought to take advantage of Snapchat's ability to post real-time events. Through this, the audiences get excited as they are offered something authentic and fun to watch.

Case Study 3

NBA has in the past taken advantage of this feature on Snapchat to impress its followers. In 2014, NBA launched its presence of the All-Star Game and aired it live on Snapchat for its followers to watch. This initiative enabled the NBA fans to watch the launch from LA and other regions across the planet. This too can work for any business that seeks to explore this option of marketing.

Partner with Snapchat's influencers

There are a number of personalities who have already made a name for themselves and have a wide range of followers on Snapchat. Just like on other related social media platforms like Facebook and twitter, influencers can play an imperative role in promoting brand awareness to their existing followers.

Bill Russell & Finals MVP Kawhi!

Use Snapchat to engage with your audience by giving them unique access to live events.

Through getting in touch with such influencers on Snapchat and partnering with them with them intention of creating brand awareness, businesses are able to take advantage of the following that these influencers already have.

Aside from taking advantage of the existing traffic from influencers on Snapchat, it is also important to note that these influencers are also skilled in producing snaps. This could be only explanation as why they are famous on Snapchat in the first place. Therefore, influencers are able to come up with spectacular snaps consisting of videos and images that can go a long way inenhancing brand awareness amongst Snapchat users.

Case Study 4

A good example of the effective use of influencers was when Sour Patch Kids had an intention of attracting more teenage consumers and reached out to an internet personality known as LoganPaul. The company came up with an impressive snap that narrated a story of Sweet and Sour embarrassing Logan. At the end of the narrative, one of them got lost in the city thereby showingan impressive suspense of teenagers.

At the end of the first story, the candy company managed to get 583k views. Surprisingly, the number of views shot to over 6.8 million at the end of the fifth story. This implied that Snapchatusers were continually interested in the stories narrated by the campaign. At the end of the campaign, Sur Patch Kids was able to register 120,000 new followers. This is thus a confirmation that telling a great story on snaps can further a business's marketing agenda to the next level.

Use Snapchat to take your audience behind the scenes

A business or company is able to make use of Snapchat to provide behind-the-scenes content to its followers. This is an ingenious way of creating a strong and engaged following. Consumers are always interested to know details of how their products are manufactured. Businesses can take advantage of this urge to capture images or videos of production process and show off with them. Additionally, a business may also capture surprise birthday parties at work and even company outings and show them to their followers on Snapchat. Through this, a business is able to not only tell interesting stories about itself but also make its followers feel incorporated and valued. This will definitely increase following.

Case study of the use of Snapchat to take your audience behind the scenes

A fashion brand called Everlane is good at this form of showcasing which has since been referred to as public relations. It has, on several occasions pulled back the curtains to take its customers through an education process while coming up with spectacular contents for its Snapchat stories. They have made use of Snapchat stories to show office tours, manufacturing warehouses and even happy hours. As a result of this, they have had enormous following from people that are interested in knowing more about the company.

Use Snapchat to take viewers behind the scenes and give them a look at your company culture.

The core value of most businesses is to connect with their target audience for their goods and services in the most convenient way. Businesses make use of a number of marketing strategies in order to meet their target margins. Snapchat can now be considered as one of the platforms that internet marketers an businesses can use to take their marketing and businesses to the next level when it comes reaching their potential consumers. While the use of Snapchat for the purpose of marketing and connecting with consumers can feel overwhelming for internet marketers and businesses, one should note that it is always gainful to come up with an effective platform that offers opportunities of connecting with target audiences. It is only through this that marketers and businesses are able to keep their clients, acquire new clients and sell more.

Printed by Libri Plureos GmbH in Hamburg, Germany